IT'S EASY TO PLAY

TOP 50 HITS

Wise Publications
London/New York/Paris/Sydney/Copenhagen/Madrid

Exclusive Distributors:

Music Sales Limited
8/9 Frith Street,
London W1V 5TZ, England.

Music Sales Pty Limited
120 Rothschild Avenue,
Rosebery, NSW 2018,
Australia.

Order No. AM952523
ISBN 0-7119-7201-X
This book © Copyright 1998 by Wise Publications

Book design by Chloë Alexander
Cover photographs courtesy of London Features International
Compiled by Peter Evans

Music Sales' complete catalogue describes thousands of titles and is available in
full colour sections by subject, direct from Music Sales Limited. Please state your
areas of interest and send a cheque/postal order for £1.50 for postage to:
Music Sales Limited, Newmarket Road, Bury St. Edmunds, Suffolk IP33 3YB.

Visit the Internet Music Shop at
http://www.musicsales.co.uk

Your Guarantee of Quality
As publishers, we strive to produce every book to the highest
commercial standards.
This book has been carefully designed to minimise awkward page turns and to
make playing from it a real pleasure.
Particular care has been given to specifying acid-free, neutral-sized paper made
from pulps which have not been elemental chlorine bleached.
This pulp is from farmed sustainable forests and was produced with
special regard for the environment.
Throughout, the printing and binding have been planned to ensure a sturdy,
attractive publication which should give years of enjoyment.
If your copy fails to meet our high standards, please inform us and we will
gladly replace it.

Printed in the United Kingdom by
Caligraving Limited, Thetford, Norfolk.

A WHITER SHADE OF PALE

Words & Music by Keith Reid & Gary Brooker

But the crowd called out for more;
And would not let her be.
The room was humming har - der
One of six - teen ves - tal vir - gins

as the ceil - ing flew a - way.
who were leav - ing for the coast,
When we called out for an -
and al - tho' my eyes were

oth - er drink
o - pen
the wait - er brought a tray,
they might just as well been closed,
And so it was that

la - ter
as the mil - ler told his tale,
that her face at first just

ghost - ly, turned a whi - ter shade of pale.
1. pale.
2. pale.

5

AGAINST ALL ODDS (TAKE A LOOK AT ME NOW)

Words & Music by Phil Collins

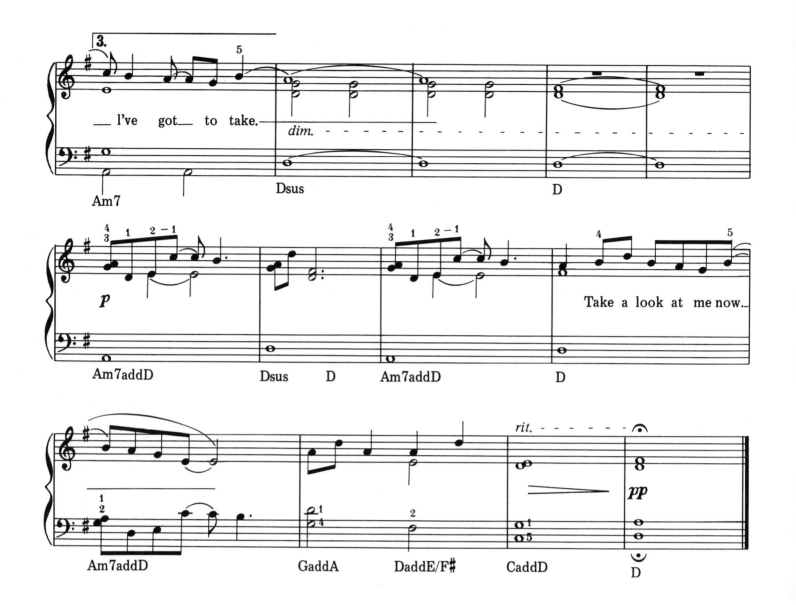

2. How can you just walk away from me,
When all I can do is watch you leave?
'Cause we shared the laughter and the pain
And even shared the tears.
You're the only one who really knew me at all.
So take a look at me now,
Well, there's just an empty space.
And there's nothing left here to remind me,
Just the memory of your face.
Well, take a look at me now,
'Cause there's just an empty space.
But to wait for you is all I can do
And that's what I've got to face.

3. I wish I could just make you turn around,
Turn around and see me cry.
There's so much I need to say to you,
So many reasons why.
You're the only one who really knew me at all.
So take a look at me now etc.
'Cause I'll still be standing here
And you comin' back to me is against all odds,
It's the chance I've got to take.
Take a look at me now.

BLAZE OF GLORY

Words & Music by Jon Bon Jovi

Moderate rock

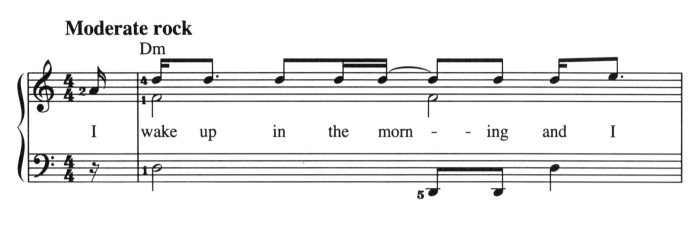

I wake up in the morn - - ing and I

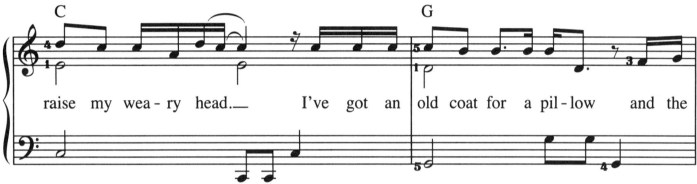

raise my wea - ry head.___ I've got an old coat for a pil - low and the

earth was last ___ night's bed. I don't know where I'm go - ing, on - ly God ___

___ knows where I've been.___ I'm a dev - il on the run, __ a six - gun lov - er, a

-ry,　　　take me　now　　　but　know　the　truth.___

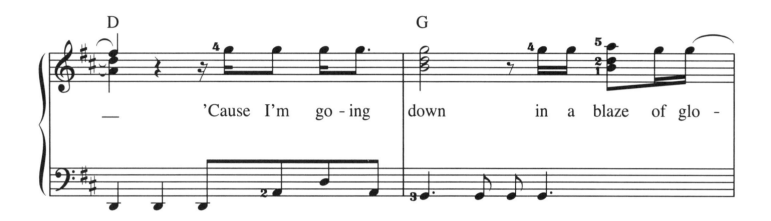

___　　　'Cause I'm　go - ing　down　　　in　a　blaze　of　glo -

- ry.　　　Lord, I　nev - er　drew　first　but I　drew　first　blood, I'm the

dev - il's　son,　　call　me　Young___　Gun.

BRIDGE OVER TROUBLED WATER

Words & Music by Paul Simon

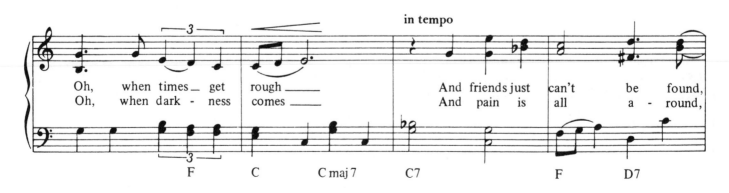

CECILIA

Words & Music by Paul Simon

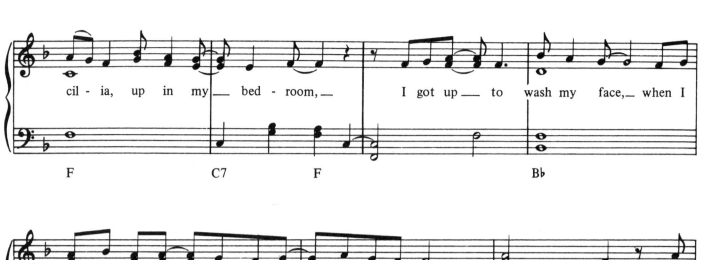

cil - ia, up in my __ bed - room, __ I got up __ to wash my face, __ when I

come back to bed __ some - one's tak - en my place. __ Cel - ia, you're

break - ing my heart, __ you're shak - ing my con - fid-ence dai - ly. __ Oh, Ce-

cil - ia, I'm down on my knees, __ I'm beg - ging you please __ to come home

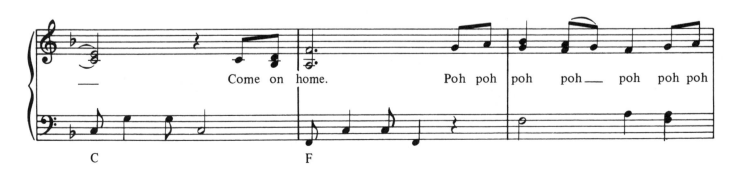

__ Come on home. Poh poh poh poh __ poh poh poh

poh poh poh poh poh poh. Ju - bi - la - tion, she loves me a - gain, I

Bb   C7   Bb F Bb F

fall on the floor and I laugh - ing. Ju - bi - la - tion, she loves me a - gain, I

Bb F C7   Bb F Bb F

fall on the floor and I laugh - ing. Oh oh oh oh oh oh oh oh oh oh

Bb F C7   Bb F Bb F

oh oh oh oh oh oh oh oh. Oh oh oh oh oh oh oh oh oh oh

Bb F C7   Bb F Bb F

rall. . . . .

oh oh oh oh oh oh oh oh. Come on home.

Bb F C7   F

(EVERYTHING I DO) I DO IT FOR YOU

Words by Bryan Adams & Robert John 'Mutt' Lange • Music by Michael Kamen

Moderately

Look in-to my eyes,___ you will see ___

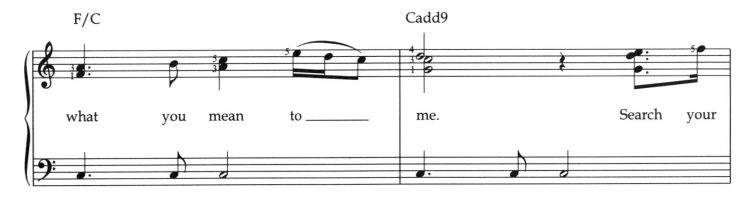

what you mean to ___ me. Search your

heart, ___ search your soul, ___ and when you

find me there you'll search_ no more. Don't tell me it's not worth try-in'

time,_____ all the way __ yeah._____

Oh you can't tell me it's not worth try - in'

for, I can't help _____ it, there's noth - in' I want

more. Yeah_ I would fight for you, __ I'd lie _____ for you, __ walk the

wire for you, ___ yeah I'd die for you. ___ You know it's true, ev'ry-thing I

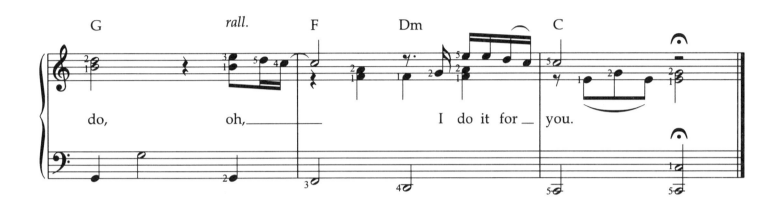

do, oh, _____ I do it for ___ you.

Verse 2

Look into your heart,
You will find there's nothin' there to hide.
Take me as I am, take my life,
I would give it all, I would sacrifice.

Don't tell me it's not worth fightin' for,
I can't help it, there's nothin' I want more.
You know it's true, everything I do,
I do it for you.

FERNANDO

Words & Music by Benny Andersson, Stig Anderson & Bjorn Ulvaeus

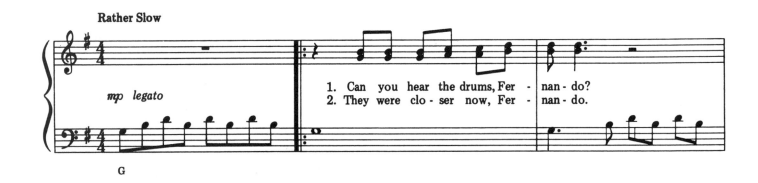

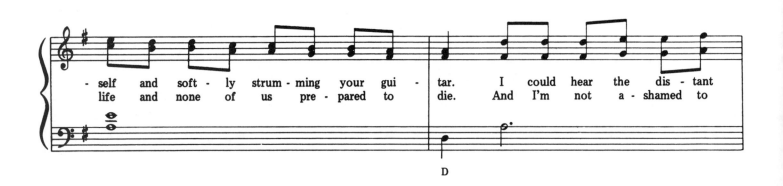

-gret.___ If I had to do the same a - gain,___ I

A7   D7   C

To Coda ⊕

would, my friend,___ Fer - nan - do.   If I had to do the

D7   G

same a - gain,___ I would, my friend,___ Fer - nan - do.

D7   C   D7   C   G   Dm7

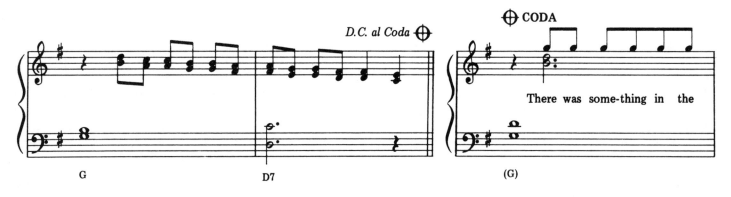

D.C. al Coda ⊕   ⊕ **CODA**

There was some-thing in the

G   D7   (G)

air that night,___ the stars were bright,___ Fer - nan - do.

D7   C   D7   G

They were shi-ning there for you and me,___ for li - ber - ty,___ Fer -

D7　　　　　　　　　C　　D7

- nan - do. Though we nev - er thought that we could lose, there's no re -

G　　　　　　Fdim　　　　　　　E7

- gret.___ If I had to do the same a - gain,___ I

A7　　　　　　　　　　　　　　　D7　　　　　C

Repeat and Fade

would, my friend,_ Fer - nan - do. If I had to do the

D7　　　　　　G

3. Now we're old and grey, Fernando
   And since many years I haven't seen a rifle in your hand;
   Can you hear the drums Fernando?
   Do you still recall the fateful night we crossed the Rio Grande?
   I can see it in your eyes how proud you were to fight for freedom in this land.

FOR THE GOOD TIMES

Words & Music by Kris Kristofferson

GOODBYE YELLOW BRICK ROAD

Words & Music by Elton John & Bernie Taupin

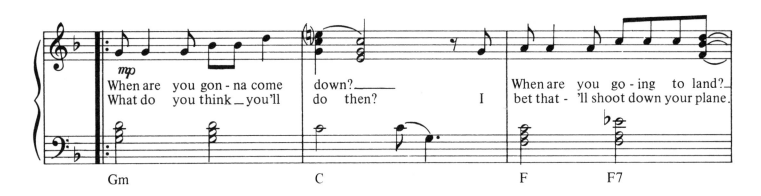

When are you gon-na come down? When are you go-ing to land?
What do you think you'll do then? I bet that-'ll shoot down your plane.

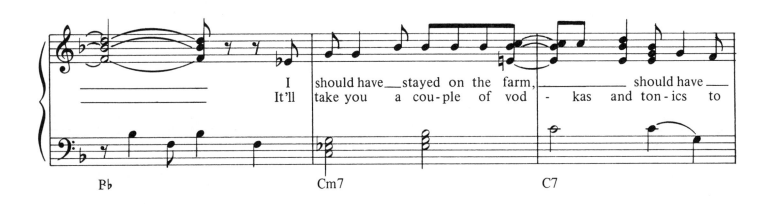

I should have stayed on the farm, should have
It'll take you a cou-ple of vod-kas and ton-ics to

lis-tened to my old man. You
set you on your feet a-gain. May-be you'll get a re-place

know you can't hold me for ev-

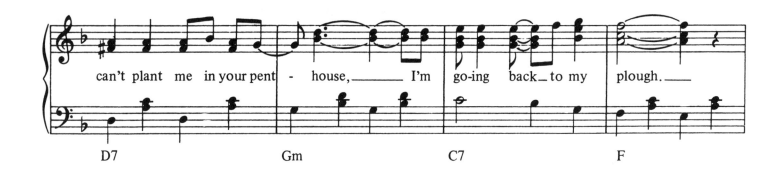

can't plant me in your pent - house, ____ I'm go-ing back__ to my plough. ____

D7   Gm   C7   F

Back to the howl-ing old owl __ in the woods, hunting the horn - y black toad.

Dm   A   Bb   Gm7   Db

Oh I've fin - 'lly de-cid - ed my fu-ture lies be - yond the yel-low brick

Eb F   Dm   F   Bb   C7

road. ____ Ah ____ ah ____

Db   Eb   Ab   Db

1   **2**

Ah ____ Ah.

C7   F   F

Ped.   *

HAVE I TOLD YOU LATELY?

Words & Music by Van Morrison

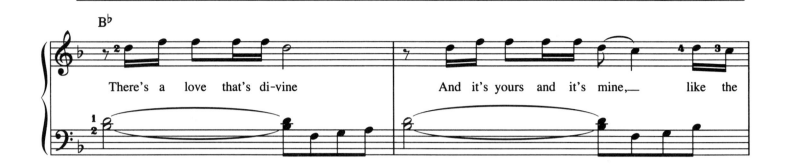

There's a love that's di-vine   And it's yours and it's mine,— like the

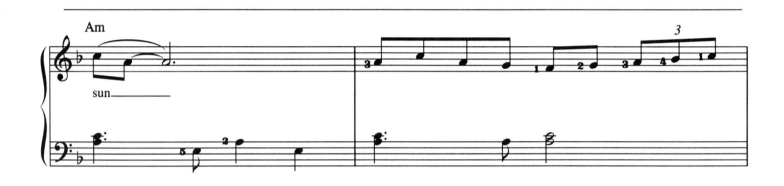

sun

At the end of the day   We should give thanks and pray to the

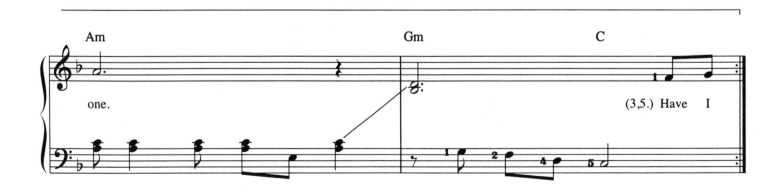

one.   (3,5.) Have   I

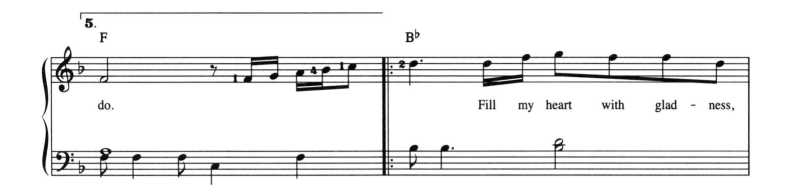

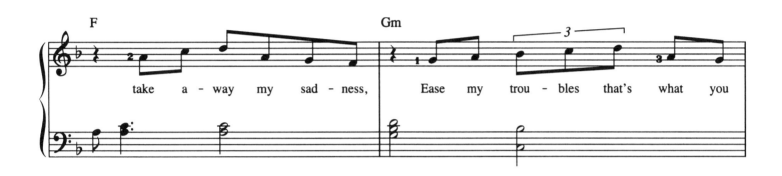

Verse 2:

Oh the morning sun in all its glory
Greets the day with hope and comfort too
And you fill my life with laughter
You can make it better
Ease my troubles that's what you do.

Verse 3: - as Verse 1

Verse 4: - Instrumental

Middle:

There's a love that's divine
And it's yours and its mine
And it shines like the sun
At the end of the day
We will give thanks and pray to the one.

Verse 5: - as Verse 1

HE AIN'T HEAVY...HE'S MY BROTHER

Words by Bob Russell • Music by Bobby Scott

If I'm la - den at all, ___ I'm la - den with sad - ness ___ that

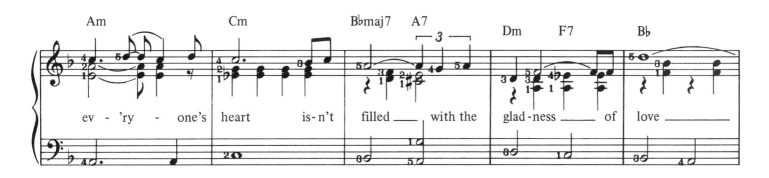

ev - 'ry - one's heart is-n't filled ___ with the glad - ness ___ of love ___

D.%. al Coda   ✠ *CODA*

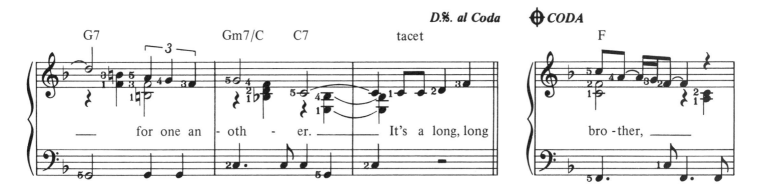

___ for one an - oth - er. It's a long, long   bro - ther, _____

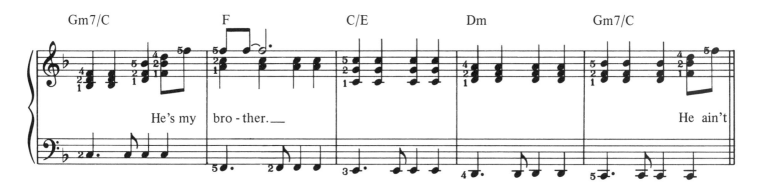

He's my bro - ther. ___   He ain't

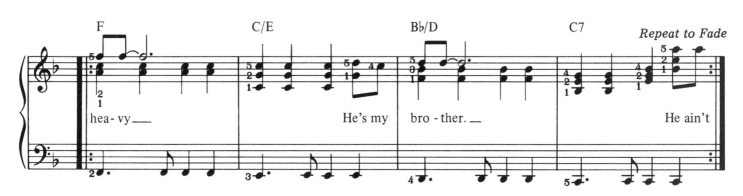

hea - vy ___   He's my bro - ther. ___   He ain't

35

I BELIEVE I CAN FLY

Words & Music by Robert Kelly

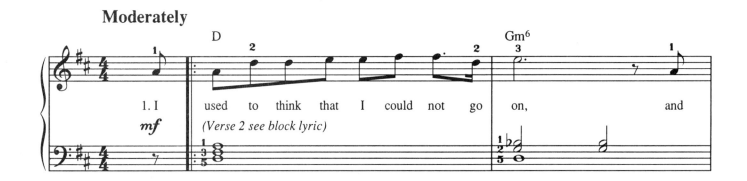

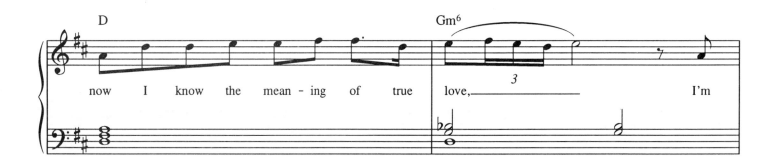

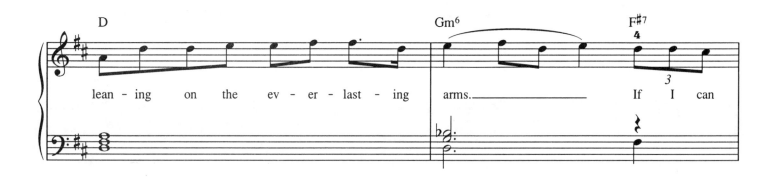

night and day,___ spread my wings and fly a - way,___ I be - lieve I can

soar, see me run - ning through that op - en door,___ I be - lieve I can

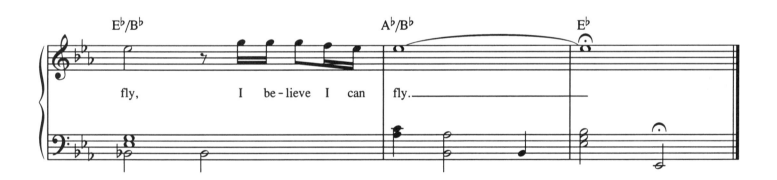

fly, I be - lieve I can fly.___

Verse 2:

See I was on the verge of breaking down,
Sometimes silence can seem so loud.
There are miracles in life I must achieve,
But first I know it stops inside of me.

Oh, if I can see it,
Then I can be it.
If I just believe it,
There's nothing to it.

I SAY A LITTLE PRAYER

Words by Hal David • Music by Burt Bacharach

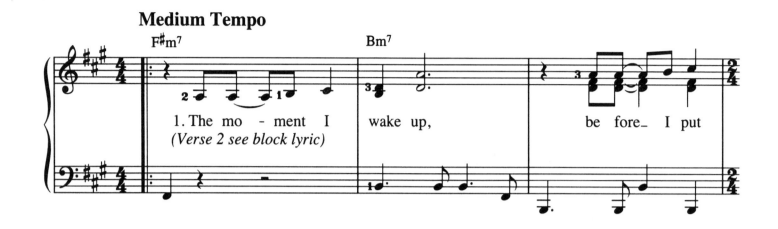

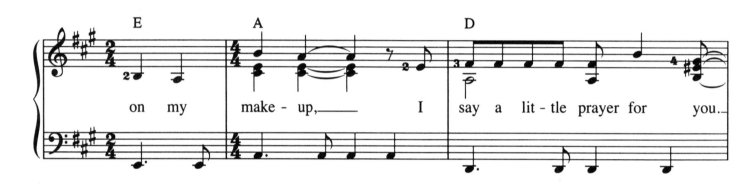

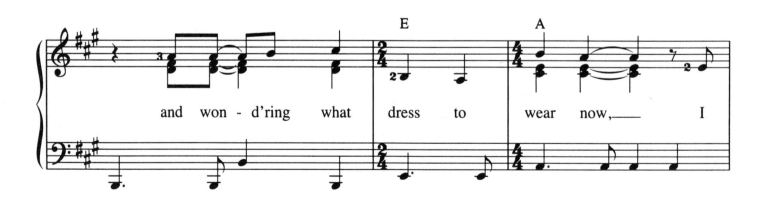

on - ly mean heart - break for me.

me.

My dar - ling be - lieve me, for me there is no one but you. Please love me too. I'm in love with you. An - swer my

42

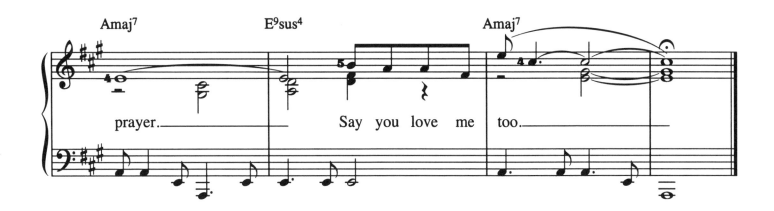

prayer. Say you love me too.

2. I run for the bus, dear,
While riding, I think of us dear,
I say a little prayer for you.
At work I just take time,
And all through my coffee break time,
I say a little prayer for you.

Forever, forever, *etc*.

I WILL SURVIVE

Words & Music by Dino Fekaris & Freddie Perren

46

I WRITE THE SONGS

Words & Music by Bruce Johnston

IMAGINE

Words & Music by John Lennon

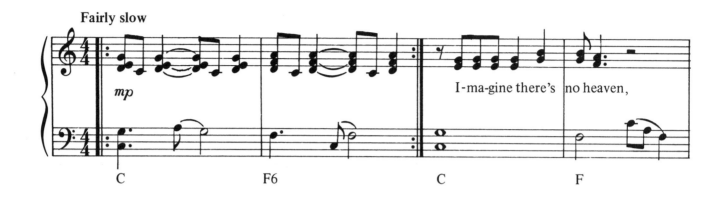

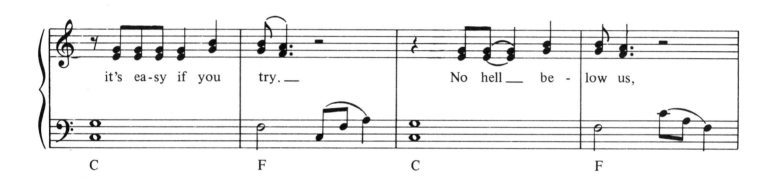

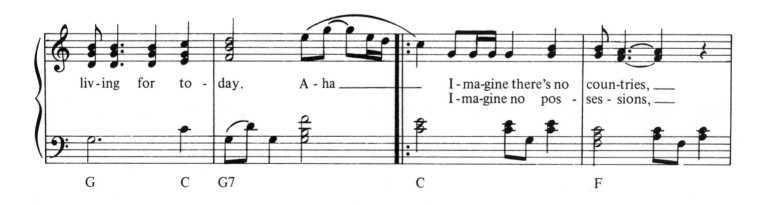

IN THE AIR TONIGHT

Words & Music by Phil Collins

I can feel it com - ing in the air tonight,_____ oh Lord._____

And I've been waiting for this moment for all my life,_____ oh Lord._____

can you feel it com - ing in the air tonight,_____ oh Lord,_____ oh Lord?

wipe off that grin, _____ I ___ know where you've been, _____ (*l.h.*) it's

D. %. al ⊕

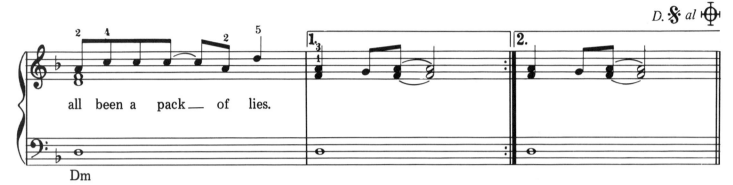

all been a pack __ of lies.

Coda

f I can feel it in the air tonight, __ oh Lord, _____ oh Lord.

Dm   C/D   B♭/D   C/D

repeat to fade

Well, I've been wait-ing for this moment for all my life, _____ oh Lord.

Dm   C/D   B♭/D   C/D

2. And I can feel it coming in the air tonight, oh Lord.
Well, I've been waiting for this moment for all my life, oh Lord.
I can feel it coming in the air tonight, oh Lord, oh Lord.
Well, I remember, I remember, don't worry,
How could I ever forget, it's the first time,
The last time we ever met.
But I know the reason why you keep the silence up,
No you don't fool me.
The hurt doesn't show, but the pain still grows,
It's no stranger to you or me.
And I can feel it etc.

LAY, LADY, LAY

Words & Music by Bob Dylan

LET IT BE

Words & Music by John Lennon & Paul McCartney

61

LOVE HURTS

Words & Music by Boudleaux Bryant

Love hurts, love scars, love wounds and mars any

heart not tough or strong e- nough to take a lot of pain; take a lot of

64

LOVE IS ALL AROUND

Words & Music by Reg Presley

Moderately

1. I feel it in my fin-gers, I feel it in my toes.

2. *(see block lyric)*

The love that's all a-round me and so the feel-ing grows

It's writ-ten on the wind, it's ev-'ry-where I go,

So if you real-ly love me, come on and let it show

Verse 2:

I see your face before me
As I lay on my bed;
I cannot get to thinking
Of all the things you said.
You gave your promise to me
And I gave mine to you;
I need someone beside me
In everything I do.

LOVE SHINE A LIGHT

Words & Music by Kimberley Rew

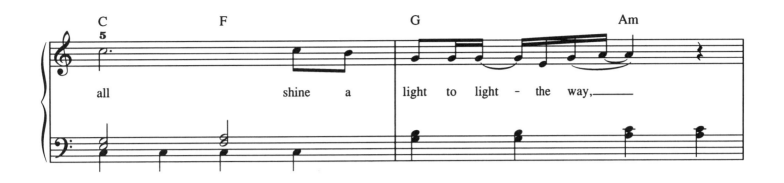

all shine a light to light the way,___

bro - thers and sis - ters___ in ev-'ry lit-tle part, let our love___ shine a light in ev-'ry

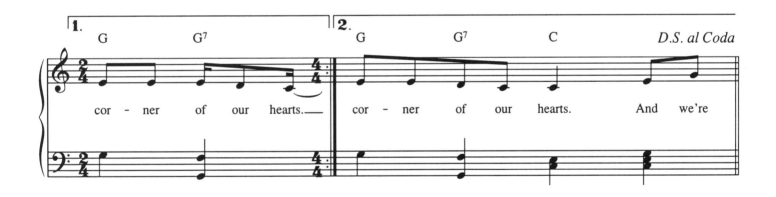

1. cor - ner of our hearts.___ **2.** cor - ner of our hearts. And we're

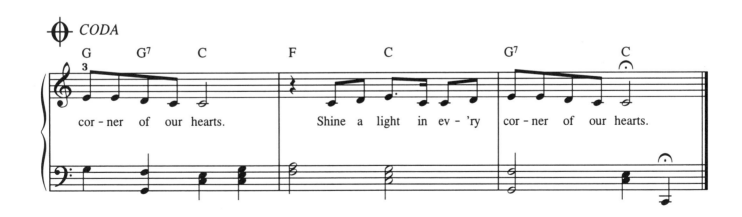

CODA

cor - ner of our hearts. Shine a light in ev-'ry cor - ner of our hearts.

MONEY FOR NOTHING

Words & Music by Mark Knopfler & Sting

Medium rock tempo

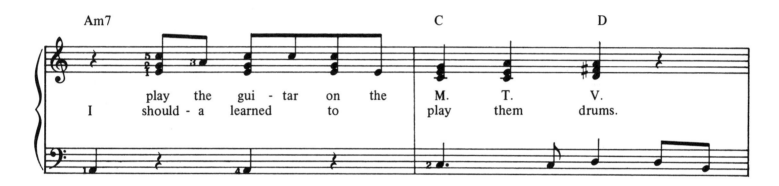

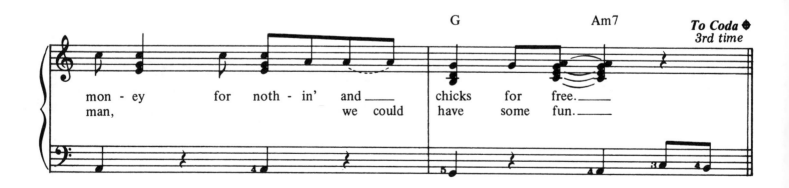

Am7   **D7**

(2.) That ain't work-in'   that's ___ the way you do it
(3.) See that little faggot with the ear - rings and the make up
(5.) And he's up there, he's mak - ing Haw - aiian noi - ses

Am7   **C**   **D**

lem - me tell ya   them ___ guys ain't dumb ___
yeah buddy that's ___ his own hair ___
bang - in' on the bongos like a chim - pan - zee ___ that

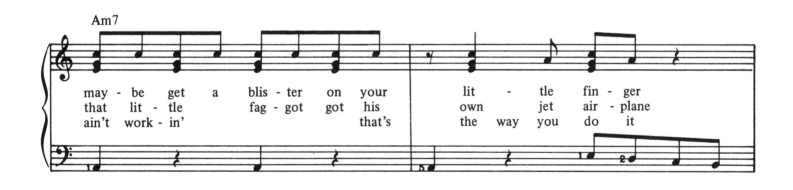

Am7

may - be get a blis - ter on your lit - tle fin - ger
that lit - tle fag - got got his own jet air - plane
ain't work - in' that's the way you do it

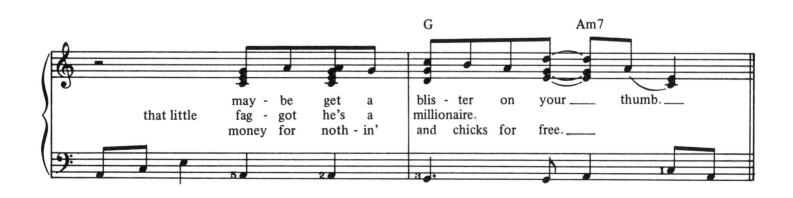

                                 G   **Am7**

may - be get a blis - ter on your ___ thumb. ___
that little fag - got he's a millionaire.
money for noth - in' and chicks for free. ___

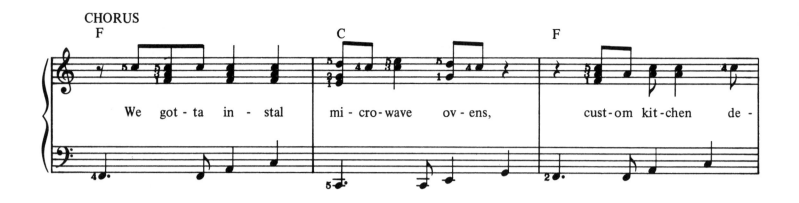

We got - ta in - stal mi - cro - wave ov - ens, cust - om kit - chen de -

liv - er - ies. _____ We got - ta move these re - frig - er - a - tors,

we got - ta move these col - our T. - V's. _____

1. | 2. 3. | D.S. twice
(2nd time to Coda ✦)

mon - ey   for   noth - in'
*spoken - ***

chicks   for   free_____

mon - ey   for   noth - in'   and

chicks   for   free. _____

PEGGY SUE

Words & Music by Jerry Allison, Norman Petty & Buddy Holly

love you, Peg - gy Sue.

C   C7   G   C   G   D

Peg - gy Sue,___ Peg - gy Sue,___ Pret-ty, pret-ty, pret-ty, pret-ty

G   Eb

Peg - gy Sue,___ oh, my Peg - gy,___ My Peg - gy Sue;

G   C   G

___ Oh, well, I love you gal,___ and I

C   G   D   D7

need you, Peg - gy Sue.___

C   C7   G   C   G   D

SHE'S OUT OF MY LIFE

Words & Music by Tom Bahler

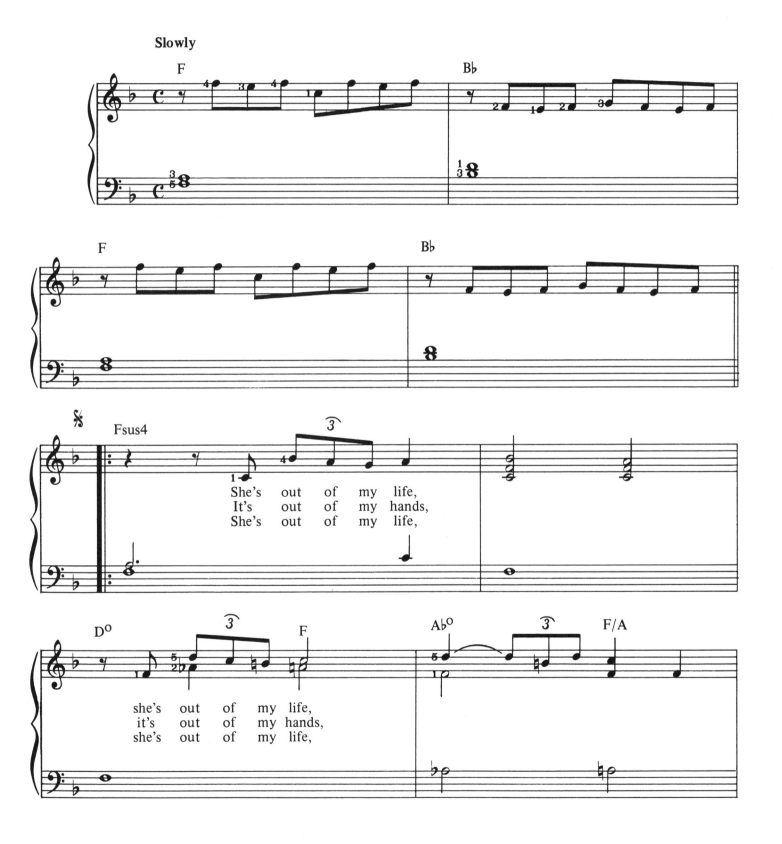

She's out of my life,
It's out of my hands,
She's out of my life,

she's out of my life,
it's out of my hands,
she's out of my life,

and I don't know whe - ther ___ to laugh or cry,
to think for two years ___ she was here,
damned in - de - ci - sion ___ and cursèd pride,

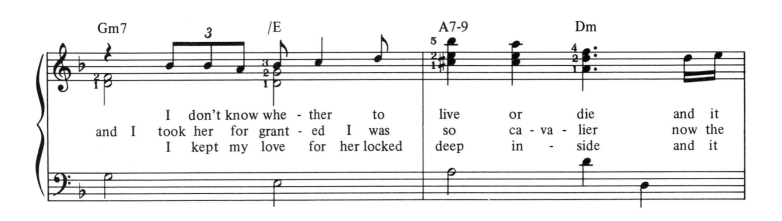

I don't know whe - ther to live or die and it
and I took her for grant - ed I was so ca - va - lier now the
I kept my love for her locked deep in - side and it

To Coda ✦

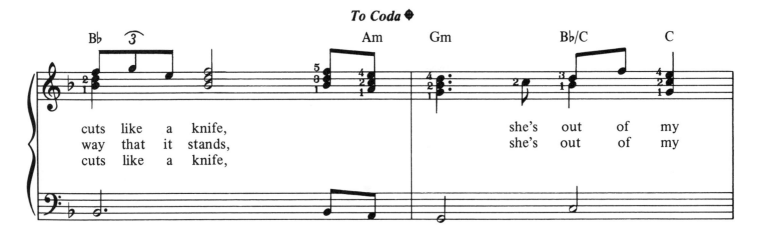

cuts like a knife,
way that it stands, she's out of my
cuts like a knife, she's out of my

life.
hands.

And so I've learned that love's not po‑sses‑sion, and I've learned that love won't wait.__ Now I've learned that love needs ex‑pres‑sion,__ but I learned _____ too late. And _____

she's out of my life.

SO FAR AWAY

Words & Music by Mark Knopfler

Here I am a-gain in this mean old town, ___ and you're so far a-way ___ ___ from me. Now where are you when the sun goes down, ___ you're so far a-way ___ from me. You're so far a-

way from me, ___   you're so far   I   just   can't   see.

You're so far a - way   from me, ___   you're   so

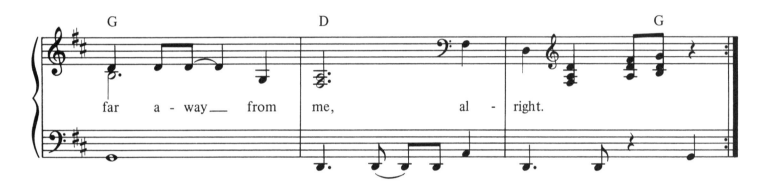

far   a - way ___ from   me,   al - right.

Repeat to Fade

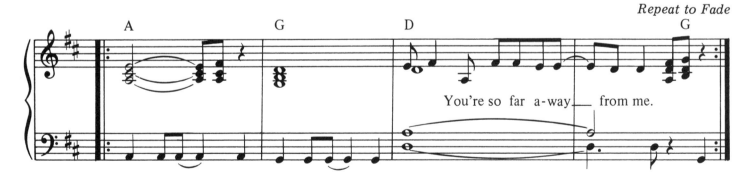

You're so far a-way ___ from me.

2. I'm tired of being in love and being all alone,
   When you're so far away from me.
   I'm tired of making out on the telephone,
   'Cause you're so far away from me.

3. And I get so tired when I have to explain,
   When you're so far away from me.
   See you've been in the sun and I've been in the rain
   And you're so far away from me.

SPICE UP YOUR LIFE

Words & Music by Geri Halliwell, Emma Bunton, Melanie Brown, Melanie Chisholm, Victoria Aadams, Richard Stannard & Matt Rowe

85

SUNNY

Words & Music by Bobby Hebb

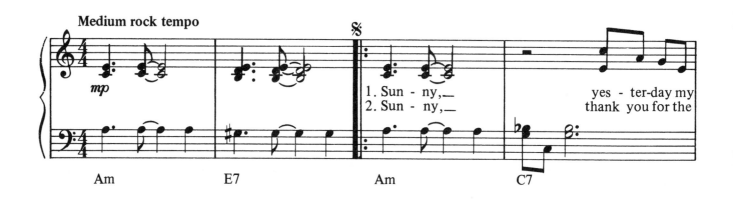

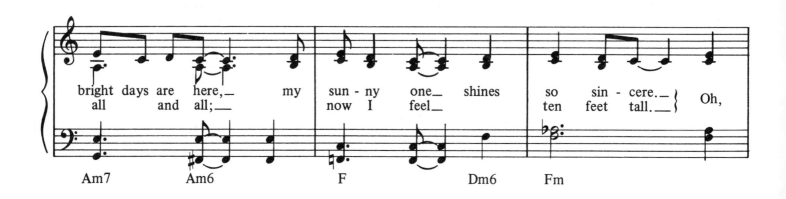

sun - ny one so true,__ I love you.__

Bm7−5   E7   Am   E7

Sun - ny,__ thank you for the | truth you've let me | see.
Sun - ny,__ thank you for that | smile up - on your | face.

Am   C7   F   F7   E7

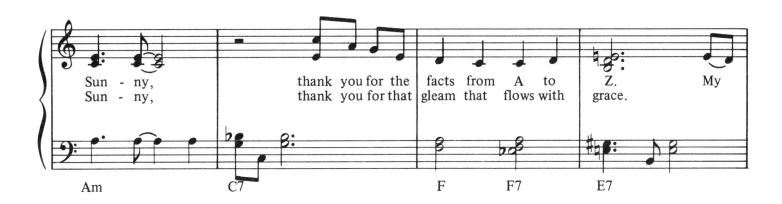

Sun - ny, thank you for the | facts from A to | Z. My
Sun - ny, thank you for that | gleam that flows with | grace.

Am   C7   F   F7   E7

life_ was torn_ like_ | wind-blown sand,_Then a | rock was formed_when | we held hands.
You're_my spark_ of__ | na - ture's fire;_ | You're my sweet_com - | plete de - sire._

Am   Am7   Am6   F   Dm6   Fm

After repeat
D.S. and fade

Sun - ny one so true,__ I love you,__

Bm7−5   E7   Am   E7

SOMETHING'S GOTTEN HOLD OF MY HEART

Words & Music by Roger Cook & Roger Greenaway

THANK YOU FOR THE MUSIC

Words & Music by Benny Andersson & Bjorn Ulvaeus

Steady four

mf

C   Am7   Dm7   G7   C   Am7   D   G7

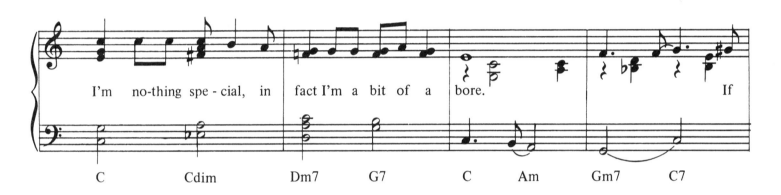

I'm no-thing spe - cial, in fact I'm a bit of a bore.   If

C   Cdim   Dm7   G7   C   Am   Gm7   C7

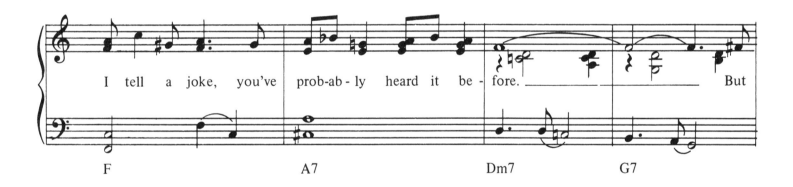

I tell a joke, you've prob-ab - ly heard it be - fore. _____ But

F   A7   Dm7   G7

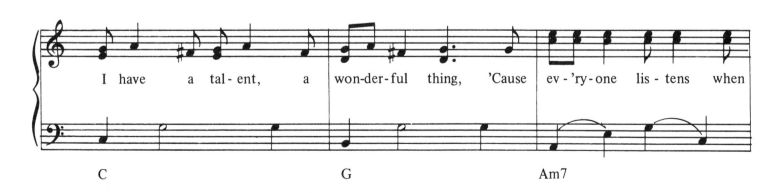

I have a tal - ent, a won-der-ful thing, 'Cause ev - 'ry-one lis - tens when

C   G   Am7

To Coda ⊕

giv - ing it to me. I've been so

G7　　　　　　　C　　Fm6　　　　C　　　　　　　Fm6

luck-y__ I am the girl with gol - den hair. I wan - na sing it out to

C　　　　　　　Fm　　Fm6　　　　C　　　　　　　Fm　　E7

D.%. al Coda

ev - 'ry - bo - dy, what a joy, what a life, what a chance.____

Am　　　　　　　　Dm7　　　　　　　　　　G7

⊕ *CODA*

me. So I say thank you for the mu - sic, for

C　　　　C7　　　　A7　　　　Dm　A7　　F

giv - ing it to me.____

G7　　　　　　　　　　　C

95

THANK YOU FOR BEING A FRIEND

Words & Music by Andrew Gold

THINK TWICE

Words & Music by Andy Hill & Pete Sinfield

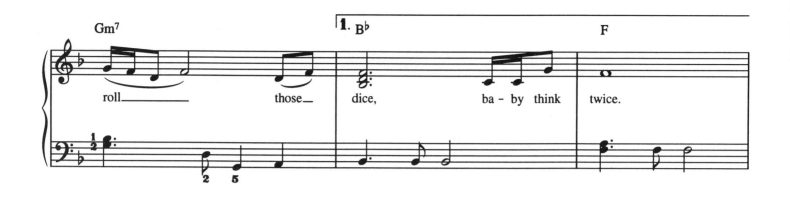

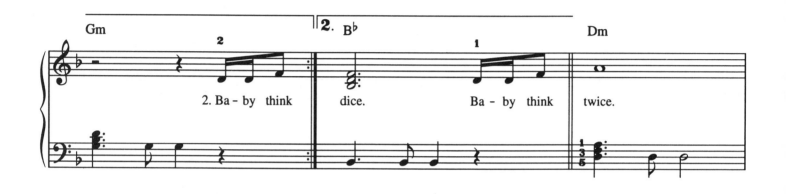

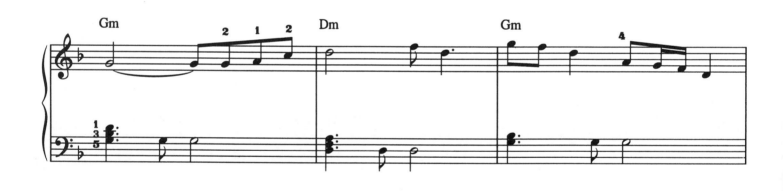

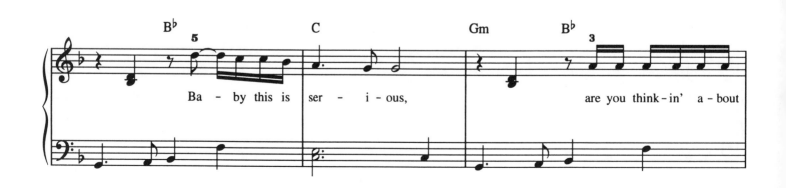

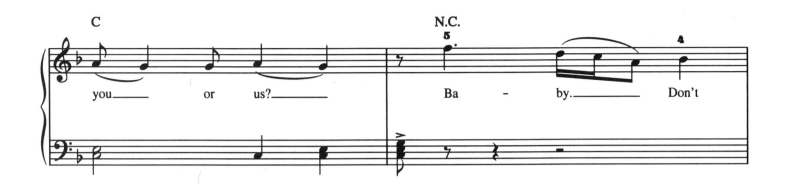

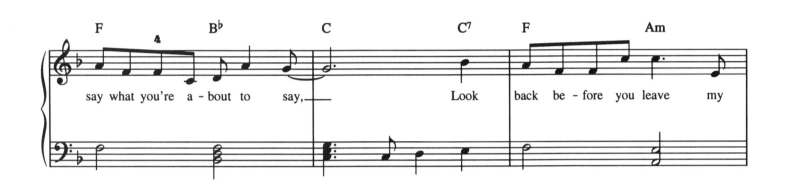

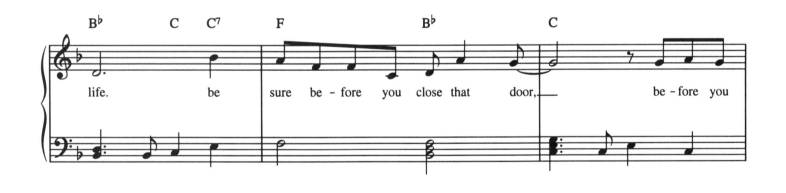

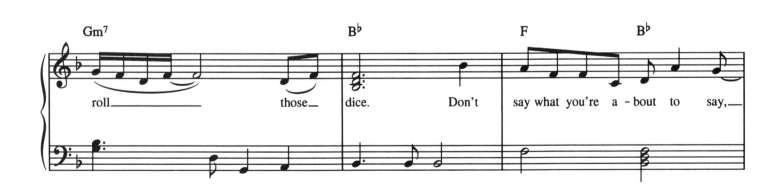

Look back be-fore you leave my life. be

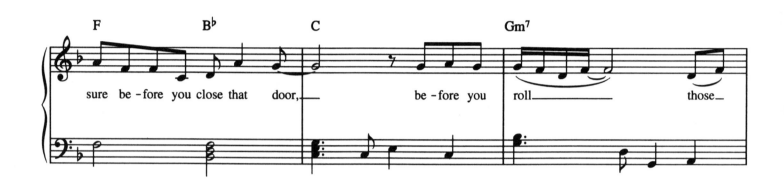

sure be-fore you close that door,___ be-fore you roll_____ those___

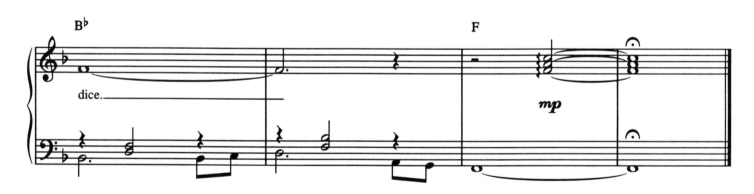

dice._____

Verse 2:

Baby think twice, for the sake of our love
For the memory,
For the fire and the faith
That was you and me.
Babe I know it ain't easy
When your soul cries out for the higher ground,
'Cause when you're halfway up
You're always halfway down.

But baby this is serious
Are you thinking 'bout you or us?

Unchained Melody

Words by Hy Zaret • Music by Alex North

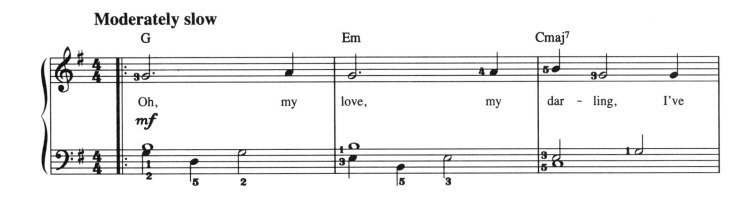

Oh,   my   love,   my   dar - ling,   I've

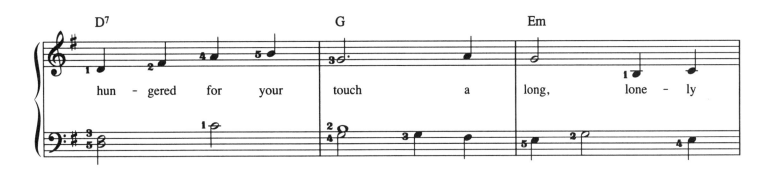

hun - gered   for   your   touch   a   long,   lone - ly

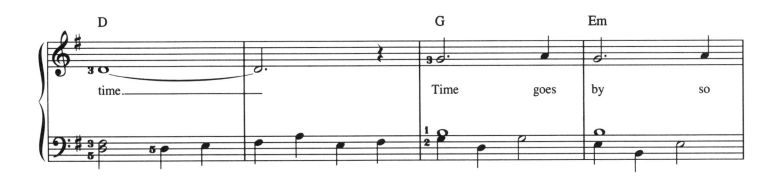

time._____   Time   goes   by   so

slow - ly   and   time   can   do   so   much,   Are

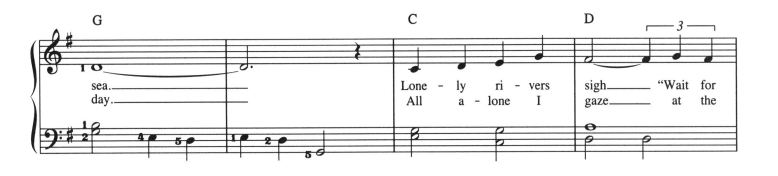

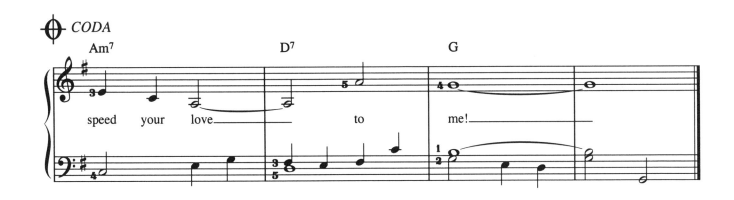

107

UNCHAIN MY HEART

Words & Music by Freddy James & Bobby Sharp

Moderately, with a beat

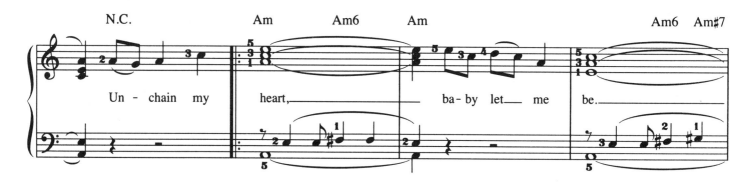

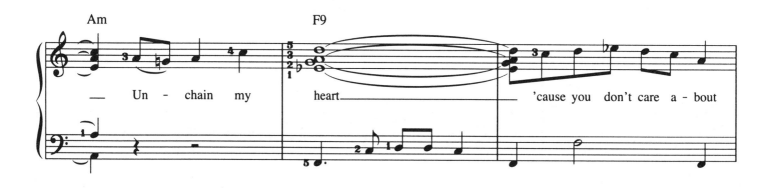

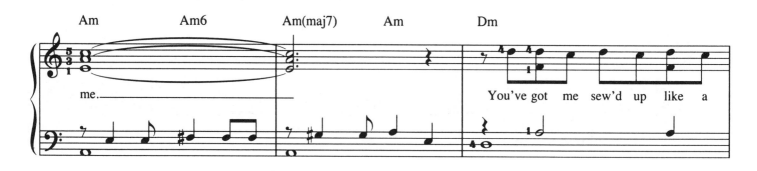

WHEN YOU TELL ME THAT YOU LOVE ME

Words & Music by Albert Hammond & John Bettis

love____ me. In a world with-out you, I will al-ways hun-ger,

all I need is your love to make me strong — er.

And ba-by

ev-'ry time you touch me, I be-come a he-ro, I'll make you safe, no mat-ter where you

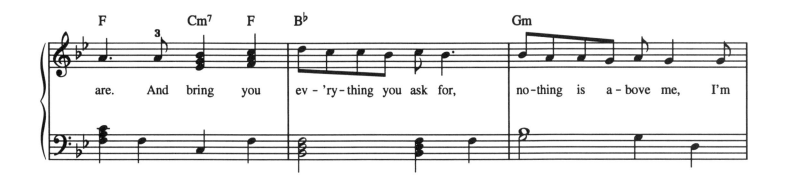

are. And bring you ev-'ry-thing you ask for, no-thing is a-bove me, I'm

shin-ing like a can-dle in the dark when you tell me that you love_____ me.

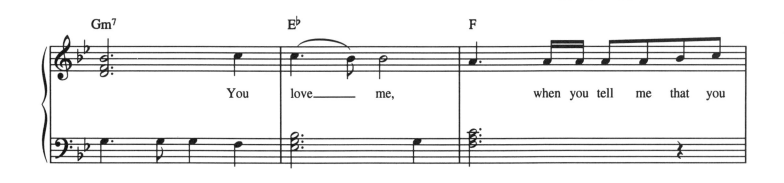

You love_____ me, when you tell me that you

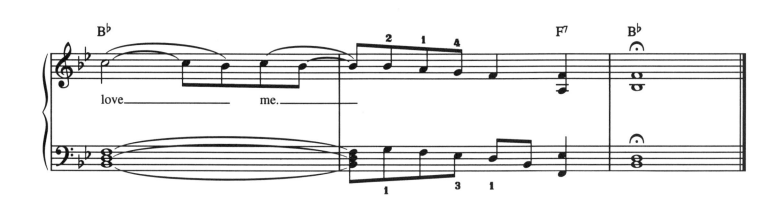

love_____ me.

WORDS

Words & Music by Barry Gibb, Robin Gibb & Maurice Gibb

And I will give you all my life, I'm here if you should call to me. You think that I don't e - ven mean a sin - gle word I say. It's on - ly words, and words are all I

WITHOUT YOU

Words & Music by Peter Ham & Tom Evans

Slowly

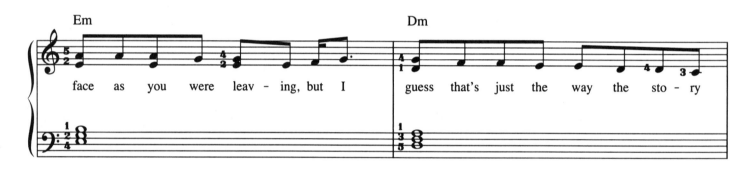

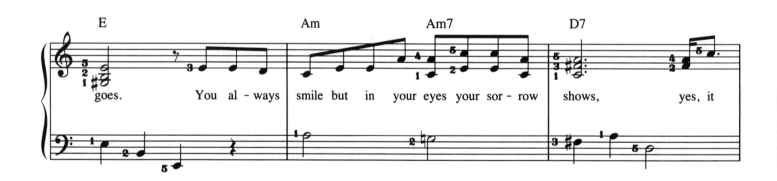

YOU MUST LOVE ME

Music by Andrew Lloyd Webber • Lyrics by Tim Rice

how do we keep____ all our pas - sions a - live as

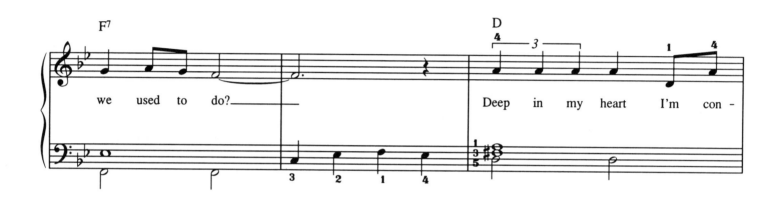

we used to do?____ Deep in my heart I'm con -

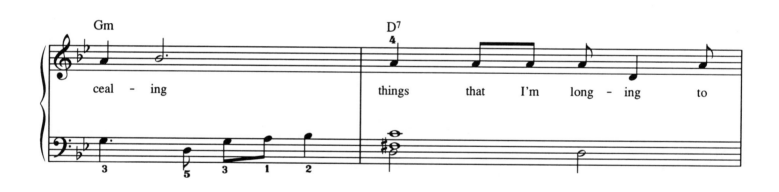

ceal - ing things that I'm long - ing to

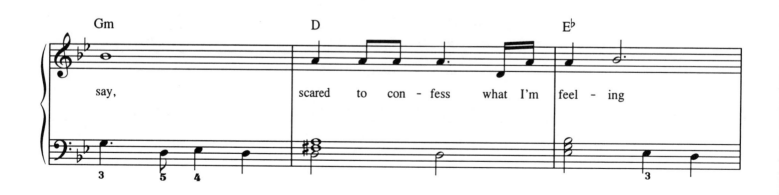

say, scared to con - fess what I'm feel - ing

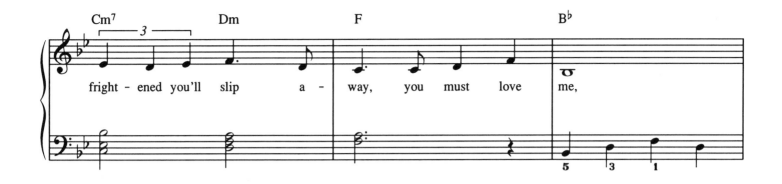

fright - ened you'll slip a - way, you must love me,

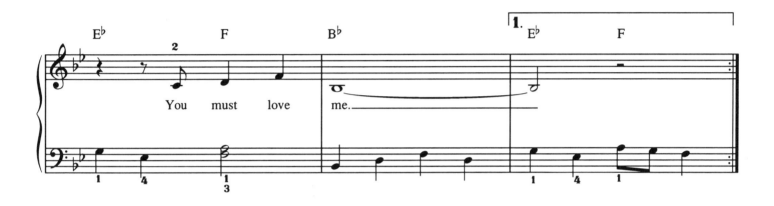

You must love me.

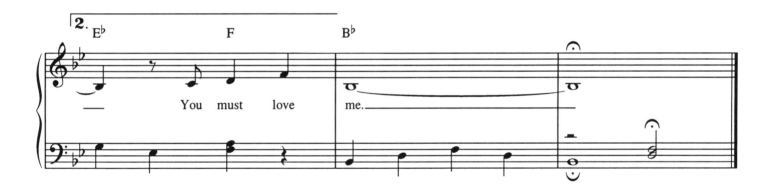

You must love me.

Verse 2: (Instrumental 8 bars)

Why are you at my side?
How can I be any use to you now?
Give me a chance and I'll let you see how
Nothing has changed.
Deep in my heart I'm concealing
Things that I'm longing to say,
Scared to confess what I'm feeling
Frightened you'll slip away,
You must love me.

YESTERDAY

Words & Music by John Lennon & Paul McCartney

Moderato

Yes - ter - day, All my trou - bles seemed so far a - way,
Sud - den - ly, I'm not half the man I used to be,

F   Em7   A7   Dm   Dm7

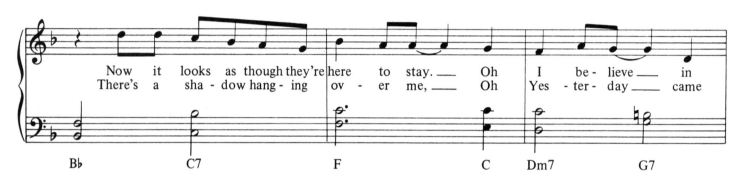

Now it looks as though they're here to stay. ___ Oh I be - lieve ___ in
There's a sha - dow hang - ing ov - er me, ___ Oh Yes - ter - day ___ came

Bb   C7   F   C   Dm7   G7

Yes - ter - day. ___ }
sud - den - ly. ___ }   Why she had to go I don't

Bb   F   Em7   A7   Dm   C   Bb   Dm

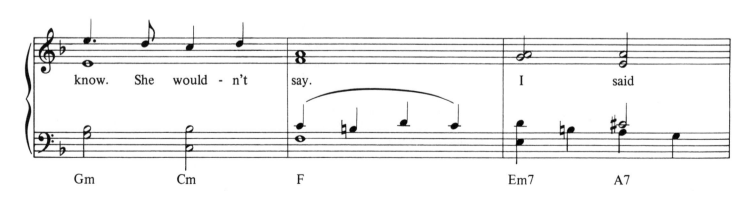

know. She would - n't say. I said

Gm   Cm   F   Em7   A7

some - thing wrong, now I long for yes - ter - day. _____

Dm   C   B♭   Dm   Gm   C7   F

Yes - ter -day,   Love was such an eas - y game to play,

Em7   A7   Dm

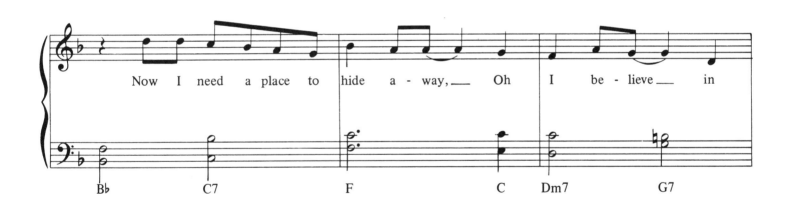

Now I need a place to hide a - way, ___ Oh I be - lieve ___ in

B♭   C7   F   C   Dm7   G7

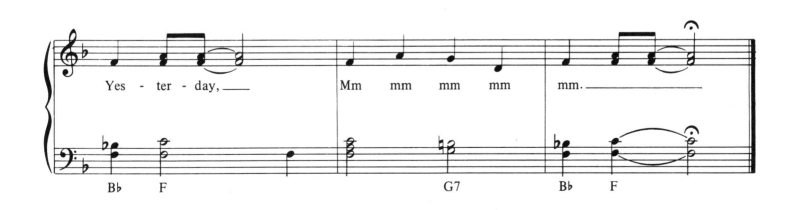

Yes - ter - day, ___ Mm mm mm mm mm. _____

B♭   F   G7   B♭   F

It's Easy To Play
The Series.

The 'It's Easy To Play' series offers you easy-to-read, simplified arrangements of music
from the world's favourite performers and great composers.
Ideal for beginners, the music is newly engraved and includes chord symbols and lyrics where appropriate.

Abba AM22195	**Chopin** AM71747	**Familiar Songs** AM36419	**Nursery Rhymes** AM37706	**Rhythm & Blues** AM33549	**The Thirties** AM68313
Bach AM71721	**Christmas Songs** AM22641	**Folk** AM18987	**Oasis** AM936276	**Cliff Richard** AM90140	**The Forties** AM68321
Burt Bacharach AM937497	**Classical Themes** AM31659	**George Gershwin** AM68511	**Opera** AM32152	**Rock 'n' Roll** AM19555	**The Fifties** AM68339
Ballads AM63025	**Classics** AM19563	**Gilbert & Sullivan** AM24225	**Roy Orbison** AM77363	**Schubert** AM71762	**The Sixties** AM68347
Ballet Music AM32939	**Classics 2** AM60252	**Hymns** AM23698	**Party Time** AM90160	**Showtunes** AM26907	**The Seventies** AM68354
Beatles NO17907	**Richard Clayderman** AM61599	**Michael Jackson** AM77348	**Piano Duets** AM62514	**Paul Simon** PS10214	**The Eighties** AM68362
Beatles 2 NO90342	**Clayderman 2** AM65921	**Jazz** AM15280	**Pops** AM27228	**Paul Simon 2** PS10883	**TV Action Themes** AM62670
Bee Gees AM77355	**Phil Collins** AM65913	**Jazz 2** AM62258	**Pops 2** AM37904	**Soft Rock** AM74220	**TV Themes** AM63033
Beethoven AM71739	**Country 'n' Western** AM19530	**Elton John** AM61714	**Pops 3** AM65905	**Songs of England, Scotland & Ireland** AM31857	**TV Themes 2** AM89468
Blues AM15264	**Disney** WD10260	**Jerome Kern** AM80268	**Pops 4** AM67596	**Cat Stevens** AM24274	**Waltzes** AM20421
Blur AM936265	**Duran Duran** AM61755	**Latin** AM18995	**Pops 5** AM77132	**Strauss** AM83791	**West End Hits** AM90097
Bon Jovi AM936287	**Bob Dylan** AM78890	**Marches** AM24969	**Pops 6** AM91212	**Swing** AM20140	**Wet Wet Wet** AM935935
Boogie-Woogie AM23706	**Duke Ellington** AM65939	**Movie Music** AM953865	**Pops 7** AM936441	**Tchaikovsky** AM82926	**Stevie Wonder** AM40007
Carpenters AM23342	**Elvis** AM20868	**Mozart** AM71754	**Pub Songs** AM69279	**The Twenties** AM68305	**...and many more!**
Children's Songs AM29489		**Music Hall** AM69287	**Ragtime** AM14143		

Available from all good music retailers or, in case of difficulty, contact
Music Sales Limited, Sales & Distribution Centre, Newmarket Road, Bury St. Edmunds, Suffolk IP33 3YB.
Telephone 01284 725725; Fax 01284 702592

www.musicsales.com